JUL 7 1983	DATE DUE	
SEP 1 3 1983	JUL 28	
JUL 1 2 1985	AUG 26	
SEP 1 2 1985	SEP 5	
DEC 6 1986		
APR 3 0	DEC 8 02	
APR 1 3		
JUL 2 4		
SEP 4		
JAN 2 1		
SEP 8 02		

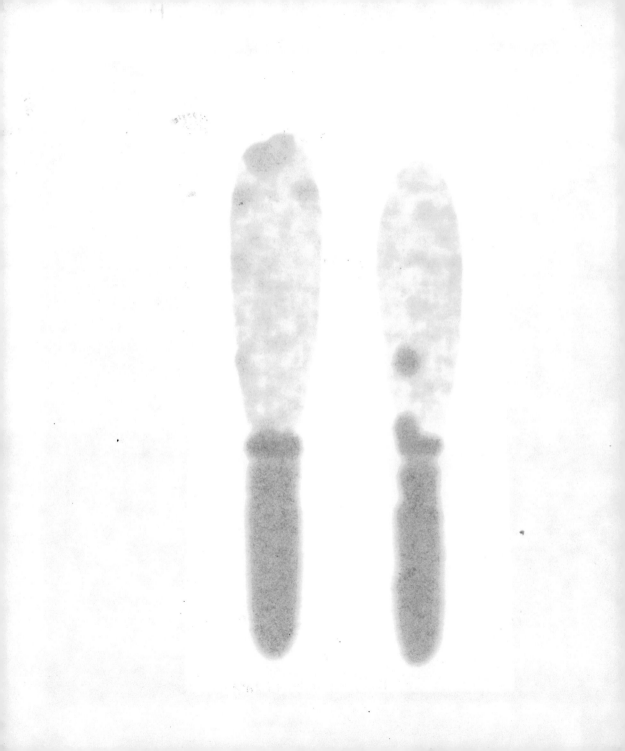

FACT FINDERS

Educational adviser: Arthur Razzell

The Cat Family

Robert Burton

Illustrated by Richard Hook
Designed by Faulkner/Marks Partnership

Silver Burdett Company

© 1976 Macmillan Education Limited

Published in the United
States by Silver Burdett
Company, Morristown, N.J.
1978 Printing

ISBN 0-382-06235-3

Library of Congress
Catalog No. 78-64654

The Cat Family

What is a Cat?

Cats are meat eaters. They use their fangs for killing prey. They slice the meat with their cheek teeth.

Cats can draw their claws into sheaths in their paws. In the dark, the pupils of their eyes get bigger to help them see.

There are 36 kinds of cat.

Eyes in dark   **Eyes in light**

—Pupil—

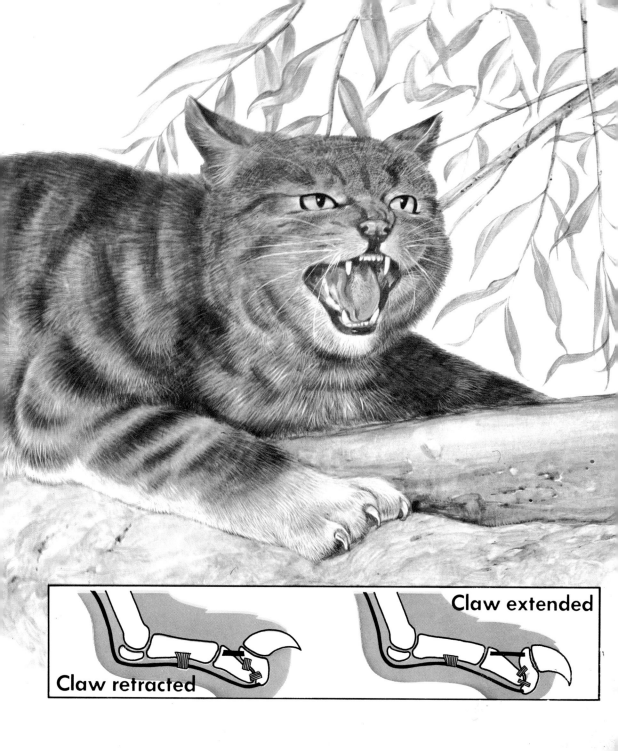

Claw extended

Claw retracted

Cats of Europe and Asia

Wild cat The wild cat looks rather like a tabby cat. It is larger, however, and has a bushy tail.

   The lynx has a short tail and tufted ears. It eats rabbits and hares. Lynxes live in Canada as well as in Europe.

Lynx

The tiger lives in Asia. The stripes on its body help it to hide in the jungle. Tigers find it hard to climb trees, but they are good swimmers. They eat mainly deer and antelopes. Old or sick tigers may even eat humans.

Tiger

Cats of America

The puma is also called the cougar.
Pumas are very good at jumping.
Baby pumas have spots, which
disappear when they grow up.

Another American cat, the
bobcat, looks like a small lynx.

The jaguar lives in South
America. It is related to the leopard.

Puma

The jaguar's fur is yellow, with rings of black spots. It can catch fish with its paws.

Jaguar

Cats of Africa

The cheetah is the fastest animal on land. It can run at 96 kilometres an hour over a short distance. Unlike other cats, the cheetah cannot sheath its claws.

The caracal or desert lynx (right) lives on open grasslands. It leaps into the air to catch birds.

The black-footed cat and the sand cat are like domestic cats. They live in deserts. Their feet have hairy soles to help them grip the loose sand of the desert.

Gazelles

The Lion Pride

A family of lions is called a pride. There are usually about ten lions in a pride. Male lions have manes. Female lions are called lionesses. The babies are called cubs.

Lions roar to tell other lions where they are. They are lazy animals and often sleep all day.

Lions live in Africa and India.

Lioness

Lion

Cubs

How Cats Hunt

Pallas's cat

A cat tries to creep up on its prey without being seen. It moves very slowly and crouches close to the ground. Then the cat pounces and kills its prey. The small ears of Pallas's cat (left) help it to hide from its prey.

Domestic cat

Leopard

The leopard climbs a tree with its prey. Then other meat-eating animals cannot steal it.

Lions usually hunt together. They sometimes catch animals as big as giraffes. Other cats hunt alone, like this domestic cat.

The ancestor of all domestic cats is the cafer cat. It was tamed by the Ancient Egyptians 4000 years ago. The Egyptians worshipped their cats and mummified, or preserved, them when they died.

Mummified cat

Persian

Siamese

The commonest cat is the tabby.
Ginger cats are also popular.
Siamese cats came from Siam, now
called Thailand. Long-haired Persian
cats need to be brushed every day.

Cafer (or bush) cat

Tabby

Ginger

The van cat of Turkey (right) likes to swim. (Most cats hate water.)

A tigon has a tiger father and a lion mother.

The snow leopard lives in the cold mountains of Central Asia. Its thick, whitish fur helps to keep it warm.

Tigon

Snow leopard

Some tigers also have white fur. The white tiger below comes from Rewa in India.

Panther is another name for leopard. The black panther is a leopard with dark fur.

The manx cat (left) has long back legs and no tail.

White tiger

Black panther

A cat takes great care of itself. It makes sure that its coat is always clean. It cleans itself by licking its fur. A cat always lands on its feet. It twists in the air as it falls (left). One cat fell 36 metres and lived.

Cats make themselves comfortable when they sleep (right). If a cat is cold, it curls up. Its tail and paws keep its nose warm. When frightened, a cat often arches its back (below). It flattens its ears and hisses with rage.

Glossary

Cheek Teeth   The teeth at the back of a cat's mouth. They are used for slicing or chewing food.

Claws   Sharp nails on the toes of an animal's paws. Claws are used to help the animal to get a grip.

Desert   A dry region where there is little rain. Few animals and plants can live in deserts.

Domestic Cat   A cat which is kept as a pet.

Fangs   The long, pointed teeth in the front of a cat's mouth. Sometimes they are called canine teeth.

Mane   Long hair on the back of an animal's neck.

Manx   A word meaning 'of the Isle of Man'. The Manx cat originally came from this island.

Mummy   A dead body, preserved by being embalmed with oil and covered with linen.

Paw   The foot of an animal.

Prey   Any animal hunted and killed for food by a meat-eating animal.

Pride   A family of lions. Sometimes there may be up to fifty lions in one pride. Most of them are lionesses with their cubs (babies).

Pupil   The black part in the middle of the eye. The pupil lets light into the eye.

Sheaths   Protective covering over the claws.

2 3 4 5 6 7 8 9 10— R —85 84 83 82